Praise for *Be Radiant*

Faced by the specter of eco-catastrophe, what can we do to ward off anxiety and paralysis? We can contemplate and celebrate, as Jacob Riyeff does in this volume, that patch of the Earth which is our patrimony. Microscopically observed and lovingly curated, these lyrics articulate, layer by layer, a Midwestern landscape and time-scape radiant with the often-hidden beauty of life. Archaeology, geology, and botany fuse in a poetry that invites readers to unearth and reverence their own inheritance in our anything but common, Common Home.

—Laurentia Johns OSB
Stanbrook Abbey, England

Jacob Riyeff's *Be Radiant* does precisely what it proclaims. Riyeff's poetry comes in a variety of styles and forms, but each poem radiates with a sense of time and place. Riyeff, like the fungi he loves so much, is a poet rooted in place. His poems reflect this rootedness. Riyeff, as a scholar, is also rooted in the English language. He weds these two in poems like "The Ruin," which is a translation of an Old English poem, and yet Riyeff places it before a burial mound in his home of Milwaukee. Consume these poems, and you will find yourself radiant as well.

—David Russell Mosely
poet and theologian

"Adaming creation beyond the Fall," Jacob Riyeff—a Blakean hybrid of poet, mystic, and illuminator—brings us a new collection that visits "Paul the hermit in the desert"—but still has time to paddle his daughter out past the breakers under an afternoon sun. We see touches of earthy Kerouac, of nature-loving Wordsworth, all against a soaring, ancient spirituality. In "Spring Ephemerals," he records, with telegraphic, haiku-like focus, intricate images of the damaged Wisconsin wilderness—dovetailing, later, with his translation of the Old English poem "The Ruin." The sequence "Leads and Diggings" excavates his own family history through voice and narrative—and extends its core sample through the strata of geologic time. This poet is a hybrid of many pasts and worlds—in other words, an American original.

—AMIT MAJMUDAR
author of *Twin A* and *What He Did in Solitary*

Be Radiant

A Sonata Pome

Jacob Riyeff

Fernwood
PRESS

Be Radiant
A Sonata Pome

©2024 by Jacob Riyeff

Fernwood Press
Newberg, Oregon
www.fernwoodpress.com

All rights reserved. No part may be reproduced
for any commercial purpose by any method without
permission in writing from the copyright holder.

Printed in the United States of America

Cover and page design: Mareesa Fawver Moss
Cover photo: Dave Hoefler
Cover art: Jacob Riyeff
Author photo: Mamie Riyeff

ISBN 978-1-59498-145-6

for southern wisconsin, my home

Contents

i. Water, Cities, Woods 13
    Old Growth 14
    De nominibus 15
    To the Milwaukee, Downtown 16
    On the Year's First Compost 17
    Morning Snow 18
    On Knowledge and Love 19
    Lake Michigan Gied 21
    Submission 22
    On Having a Daughter 23
    Milwaukee Protests June, 2020 24
    On First Concert at the
        Bradley Symphony Center, Milwaukee 25
    Sketch for Desert Fathers 26
    Marin 27
    Big Sur 28
    Haight Pome 29
    Bogquilt 30
    The Night 31
    On Free Organ Concerts in
        Milwaukee's East Village 32
    Martin's Woods 33

On Picking a Spotted Touch-Me-Not...34
On Reading the Biography of Henry I: A Triolet..............35
Freude: On Hearing Beethoven's 9th Symphony
    after a Two-Year Pandemic Delay..36
A Pentecost Sonnet 37
June Sketch..38
On Being the Tooth Fairy..39
Holy Resurrection Monastery... 40
Fen and Fastness: Images..41
Beach-glass...42
The Watermen: Door County Scenes...................................43
To a Whale Bobbing Rhythmically in the Surf................ 46
Jefferson County Highway Lunes 47
For My Father...48

ii. Spring Ephemerals 51
    Spring Ephemerals 52
        cudahy woods 52
        warnimont bluff fens, a...52
        warnimont bluff fens, b 53
        kurtz woods..53
        kewaskum maple-oak woods..53
        milwaukee river floodplain and forest..........................53
        jackson marsh, a...53
        jackson marsh, b...53
        tichigan springs and fen, a...54
        tichigan springs and fen, b...54
        tichigan springs and fen, c 54
        bratt woods, a (supplementum series) 54
        bratt woods, b (supplementum series)..........................54
        donges bay gorge, a (supplementum series) 54
        donges bay gorge, b (supplementum series)..............55
        man mound park (supplementum series) 55
        the lower narrows 55
        durward's glen (supplementum series) 55
        riveredge creek and ephemeral pond, a.......................55
        riveredge creek and ephemeral pond, b......................55

A Cry of Lunes 56
    moraine lune 56
    december lune 56
    vigils word-lune 56
    i-94 east lune triptych 57
    benedictine lune 57
    redwood lune 58
    big sur lune 58
    empire prairie lune 58

iii. Lows/*Hlæwas* 61
  Deer Camp 62
  The Ruin 63
  Intaglio 65
  The Kviða of Helgi Hundingsbane
    (Final Scene) 66
  Weland the Smith 69
  Leads and Diggings:
    A Conglomerated Narrative 71
    I. The Poetics of Extraction 72
      Janesville, 2007 72
      Vinegar Hill, 1933 74
      Vinegar Hill, 1865—Ludwig Schaeber 76
      Stratford, 1910 78
      Vinegar Hill, 1851—Alice Thomas Hocking 79
      Millbrig Hollow, 1885 81
    II. The Night Heron's Call 83
      Between the Mississippi and Lake Michigan,
        anytime in the later Holocene 83
      Shallow Ocean, ca. 460-420 million years ago ... 84
      The Confluence of the Yellow and
        Mississippi Rivers, ca. 1,000 years ago 87
      Man Mound Park, 2018 and ca. 1,000 years ago ... 87
      Carwynnen, ca. 3,900 BC 89
      Rock River Valley below Lake Koshkonong,
        ca. 16,000-13,000 years ago 90

Marquette County, 2020 93
III. The Lions of Time... 94
Milwaukee, 2020 94
Gwillanwarthas, 1841—Thomas Hockin 95
Philadelphia, Oct. 7, 1828—Ludwig Schaeber 95
Durward's Glen, 1866... 98
Janesville, 2020... 99
IV. Till and Beds 102
December 2020, along Highway 51 102
Below Fulton, early 1800s 105
Milwaukee, 2020 107
Johnson Hill Kame, Sheboygan County, 2021 107
December 4, 1962, Edgerton 108
Maple Creek, 1881 110

iv. The Monadnock Apostrophes:
Baraboo Hills, Wisconsin... 113
i. The Rock Hermitage, Durward's Glen 114
ii. Baxter's Hollow 115
iii. Alpine Diner 116
iv. Pewit's Nest... 118
v. The Lower Narrows 119

Acknowledgments and Thanks.. 121
Title Index 123
First Line Index 129

accedite ad eum, et illuminamini
—Psalm 33:6

i. Water, Cities, Woods

thru birdstart
  wingdrip
    weed-drift

of the soft
  and serious—
    Water

—Lorine Niedecker, "My Life by Water"

Old Growth

—Cudahy Woods, Mother's Day 2020

Sleet and stiff breeze cold about the ears,
the children tramp along, rejoice in chilled mud
streaming down the path and pooling in booted puddles.
Mayapple stands spy our single-file advance,
bog onion hooding its glare in spare snatches
underfoot as the water gathers, saturating the woods.
The pulse of green and brown so dark it's black to the eye,
trout-lilies radiate tepals, colonizing the forest floor
in all directions, surrounding us, enveloping our bodies,
our feet, our eyes with bashful, downturned blushing blooms.
They grow silent, perched and tranquil on basal leaves.
Their forebears were here long before ours, spreading, spawning,
waxing, filling the hillsides, worting the leaf litter.
And they endure, praising all the echoes of trees
streaming through trillium, cowslip peering down the creek,
calling with floral voices, the rattle of branches overhead
for years on years as bulbs wait in papery husks.

De nominibus

We argue about bellwort in this late-night
pizza joint, sheltered
from February cold. Well,
not so much bellwort itself

as the value of knowing its common name.

You say it's so we can ignore
the *mysterium* that is the verdant
respiring cellulose and chlorophyll
itself, and so, a sham.

I say it's so we're familiar
with bell-shaped pendent beauty,
impossible to ignore as we rush by,
obliged to say hello
to an old friend we recognize:

Adaming creation beyond the Fall.

I suppose our assumptions work
toward the same attentive end.
The familiar can breed contempt—
still: their names on my tongue.

To the Milwaukee, Downtown

once you had banks
not tall steel ribs
holding back the grass
from your swelling roll

On the Year's First Compost

the children open eyes wide
as gray winds billow thru the alley.
finally they believe that our food
becomes deep rich earth—
a transformation they'd not accept
on faith. the centipedes and earthworms
rejoice in my work as i bucket
up their troping of rebirth.
mulberries fall round about,
dark corpuscular rain. and i trowel
in the compost, feeding the mouths of corn,
tobacco, high balancing begonias
that dance like pink chandeliers in the draft.
a mama thrush sneaks in the maple
leaves above, kids scuttling
aswirl as i dig. one lone
squash blossom flashes out
in sudden relief, life from death—
shock of yellow on black of earth.

Morning Snow

chaotic flurry
white against brick and red pine
february still

but still here behind the pane

On Knowledge and Love

*—Schlitz Audubon Society during the
Pandemic of 2020*

A solitary tom strolls
over moss-blanket timbers,
thru the underbrush and trunks.
I've never known the wet
beauty of bogs and swamps,
marshes and fens, mudsunk
logs like shipwrecks in the fern
drowned deep in the mire,
radiance of cowslip against the black
rot of last year's leaves.
My hand brushes over beads,
a red-tasseled *mala*
left in my raincoat's pocket
on retreat in Big Sur.
And these pines sing to those pines,
growing beside their seas.

OM Abba OM

Gobbles sing out around us,
they continue their halting trek
thru the dank duff of spring.
The blue-white spangle
of a perching tree swallow
welcomes us to the prairie,
children and turkeys calling
to each other across the grass.

OM Abba OM

There are those who say knowledge
is prior to love, and those
who say God can be excepted,
because God is prior.
I wonder if the earth
should be excepted too.
But then I breathe the fog
in off the lake and hear
the birds' cacophonous harmony
and know, like God, the earth
is prior. And so, we love
and are one, even
when we're too dull to know.

OM Abba OM

Lake Michigan Gied

we're digging sand and stone at the shore
welter of waves wastes our efforts
dripping and joyful—the day's lake-play

Submission

dark canyon walls shining moonglow
flood the mind in low steady lamplight.

all the poems and songs tempting death
like a coolly arched glass of pinot noir
sitting gently atop the stout and looming
bookcase my grandfather built
to house his paperback novels and guides
to biblical hebrew he longed to master before
he began his long surrender to the cancer that devoured
his lungs. a lone cigarette case that fills the eye
like sunshine, like seascapes, like bold oil paintings
of fruit—pears and grapes deep in mourning—
parts of banjos and guitars scattered like sand
on tables, tv stands, any spare surface.
and hide glue congealing in small coffee tins
as we laugh and heckle in cellars, glance downward
so as not to meet one another's gaze. and will
the evening hour call our bluff, as we drape
legs and backs over crumbling consignment store furniture?

will it see through our skin, our bones? the very
air knows we're frightened like small children
hugging stuffies in their nest-built beds. and will
the evening hour call our fearful bluff?

On Having a Daughter

Beneath an afternoon sun
I paddle my daughter out,
out past the breakers.
She smiles, her hair falling
across her cheek askance,
the jeweled waves glinting
in her eyes. And this is where
I would keep her—out
beyond the turmoil near shore.

But, bobbing with her in the sea-surge,
I know she won't stay here.
She will stumble in the backwash,
circled by flotsam, mangled
fish carcasses, driftwood
stumps too large for play.

Beneath an afternoon sun
I paddle my daughter out,
out past the breakers,
and we find a moment's liquid
pleasure, cheating time
for her smile. And I would have her
stay here, out past the breakers.

But we have to be getting ashore.

Milwaukee Protests June, 2020

milwaukee's smell
        absent today
nothing to do
        but listen

On First Concert at the
Bradley Symphony Center, Milwaukee

—"A man's attitude to life." (Feb 20, 2022)

O Edward Elgar, did you see our faces
rapt in darkness, hearts attuned to your cello
as you lay upon your deathbed, traces
of joy accompanying the low and mellow
tones the strings invite our ears to hear
amid glissando runs to keep the mind
and body clear? You cursed its weak premiere
but here a hundred years past you find
a willing crowd to celebrate your movements
as you lay in Worcester gasping for air,
from lyric to rondo, joyful fulfillment
in sonic pattern, virtuosic fare.
Could you see, in your final agony,
our festival of superfluity?

Sketch for Desert Fathers

—New Camaldoli Hermitage

Paul the hermit in his desert
or Guthlac of Crowland in his fen,
they gather the birds to nest
on their outstretched hands and shoulders
as if roods animate and bearded,
their friendship a mirror of Eden.
Blue joy on the bush,
on the ground outside our cell,
perched heavily on my shoe.

These Stellar's Jays avian miracles—
that, or they want our food.

Marin

Relinquo vos liberos ab utroque homine

The towhees are singing their whirring song,
and canyon breeze wafts in cool.
In bed reading Ferlinghetti,
"Pictures of the Gone World," and resting
from redwood strolls and salt marsh flankings,
our naked legs framing the bed.
And Marin is here whether I am or not,
the flowers and fog, the churches and shops,
the succulent scent of spice and sea.
We've walked and keep on walking. We've called
and heard nothing for years but the silent heart;
the sinews that lift the soft macchiato
to satisfied lips up from Washington Square
will fail and these vehicles eventually halt.
And we're in the canyon in San Rafael,
waiting to roll in dream to her bay,
to find the crucified one's embrace
at the bottom and await the body's waking.

Big Sur

The man swiveling disembarks
quickly at this Hwy 1 oasis
Seven o'clock shadow, paper in hand
past us seated in morning dapple,
burned out and wanting to get where he's going
Where is he going? Going to America,
his children pilgriming to celestial Jerusalem?
Heated! Confused! Hopeful!
Out the door with caffeine in hand
He's cool He's here He's off
down the coast.

Haight Pome

talking virgins over crepes
and coffee gathering surface fat:
reading kerouac's "the moon"
and a tree slaps me beautifully
in the face with its falling message—
this is the diamond burliness
i've been waiting for! charmed
by the bay and god's eye.

Bogquilt

blue goose road at night
cuts thru bog country
streams of leaves
flow the road
and moats dogs
aflight, all
of them. gray
light purpling
the air. vertigo
round cedar-lined
curves. watching
for deer—
there—the moon
shines over acid
water, pitcher-plant
relics, my brow.

The Night

ecce tabernaculum dei cum hominibus et habitabit cum eis

broadsides stapled to telephone poles
and electricity of stars in cities:
tonight i do not care for sleep
tonight you don't want me, and you school me
in restraint, so i will write
this poem and dream of pinochle and port
the heat in my forehead enough
to raze this block and exult in that starlight
the one who made me has come tonight,
to lay in my tabernacle—we have dined

On Free Organ Concerts in Milwaukee's East Village

Free organ music here
on the East Side. Gray afternoons
of autumnal equinox, fresh fallen
leaves. So few here in this temple,
eyes shifting in heads as Bach
swirls and glints about Romanesque
archways, the rose window hidden
behind rows of pipes, the Sacred Heart
refracting the bare light of None.
Lilting chords fuguing along
on the eardrum remind the harmony in bones,
that we live and breathe. The upper register
presses ossicles to proclaim that the Lord
is my Rock and in him there is no wrong.
Wind cascades in rounds tripling
back, too much for the mind to linger
elsewhere. And so we listen—the bass's
throb excites the nerve endings,
the soul that much richer. I sit
toward the back on Mary's side,
not knowing a thing about organ music—
not to speak of, anyway—
and it doesn't even matter. Here
we have beauty and we have it for free.
And no one can rob these glistering melodies
from our ears, our buttocks on wooden benches,
our spines. There is nothing and nowhere
but this rush of harmony now, crystalizing
the mass of consciousness with metal, air,
the depression of bone and blood and flesh
on polymer in strict, tempered proportion.

Martin's Woods

logs drowning
in seas of moss
know something i don't

On Picking a Spotted Touch-Me-Not

This orange-speckled cup
with alternating leaves,
yellow petals shining
in the late-summer light,
floods my field of vision
and reminds me of my wife, of all
the trouble of ten years,
of my cousin sitting hatted
and hooded in Cape Cod sand
explaining her preferred sleeping
arrangements, of the gannet's bath
welling and minute crabs slinking
sideways underfoot as small
children gape, scrambling
to beat the incoming tide
in canals crumbling amid foaming
swirls of sea-stream. And the sandstone
coils around our hearts near quartzite
props polished with careful footfalls.
My nephew lashes the air for a butterfly
billowing like a lamb made of light itself,
no regard for safety or our plans.
And my son cries in the forest up ahead
angling a bluff path, my nerves
like Achilles and Priam sitting
in their hut by the sea, lapped
by waves of sorrow and release.

On Reading the Biography of Henry I: A Triolet

In the failing evening's light I read
of England's early, sturdy kings.
To rest—for rest is what I need—
in the failing evening's light I read
of Henry and of William. Here we're freed
of royal yokes, but as Vespers rings
in the failing evening's light, I read
of England's early, sturdy kings.

Freude: On Hearing Beethoven's 9th Symphony after a Two-Year Pandemic Delay

—June 16, 2022

The master couldn't hear his work,
but here we are listening together—
where the flowing waters meet—
to Beethoven's final symphony.
These contrasts and crescendos at times too much:
a smile releases the mind's discomfiture.
A trumpet player drinks some water,
waiting for his chance, the ringing choir
is a morose tribunal peering down
on the merrymakers, their glee-woods.
The stilted clap at movement's end
persists, and no one seems to mind.
We've all waited years for this scherzo—
let them have their gratuitous applause!
Whatever abyss will welcome us,
we have this joy together now.

A Pentecost Sonnet

South of Port des Morts we find ourselves,
the wren is holding high-ground, loon the low.
Forget-me-nots and downy violets' bells
top the bluff where new aspens grow.
The Spirit descended like tongues of fire today,
a driving wind on *Michigami*, sporting
with pelicans and pines, licking sand and clay
as the rock and soil we can't see are forming.
The trees ring us round as the *Veni creator* resounds,
drawing all things, all things to Himself. The ferns
hang low, blessing their pines and marking the bounds
of the soft curving bay. Under the flight of Forster's terns
the shores and waves of the Great Water say
their Vespers as we avoid the great noise we've made.

June Sketch

first cool breeze of summer
too much gin
too much gin

open the cellar door
mulberries under bare feet

down the too-steep stairs

On Being the Tooth Fairy

the dollar bill refuses to yield
as i struggle to stay quiet in the dark,
taught and rigid, cramping down the sides
of the small wooden box a cousin
gave you when you were the size of a melon.
these years, six and thirty-six now,
and i can't believe you don't wake up
here in the dark as we pretend.
your brother grunts, turns like an otter
in the lower bunk, your hair across your face.
i'm so worried i'll spoil it for you—
that you'll start awake and know the secret—
why do i care? why do i write now
by light from a used advent candle,
the scent of sulfur still in the air
as your mother throat-breathes in her sleep?
you've done this to me. it's vital tonight
that i play the fairy, so you can believe.

2-20-19
Milwaukee's East Village

Holy Resurrection Monastery

—St. Nazianz, WI

the hall lined with cyrillic inscriptions
i can't begin to grasp, darkness
reigns for now. the scuttling of monks
and visitors is a song in the quiet before dawn.
the icons demand kisses, and always
more incense, the young deacon a whirling
seraph, sash in hand. now they're clapping
up and down the halls upstairs,
the call to awaken, semantron pulses
haunt the p.a., the call to prayer.
dark figures moving in the dark.

12-29-18

Fen and Fastness: Images

—Tichigan Fen and Springs, 2020

up from the fen sedge
flies dart the dapple
limits human and geological
*

arboreal chipmunks
and spring runs seeping for oaks
to make the mire-bank grow
*

columbine hangs on
spring splash under tree song
old logs into soil
*

pine-topped esker
gravelling creatures in the wind
lightning bug napped in leaf
*

against the blue expanse
an egret white, sublime
climbing, climbing as we ground
*

a bittern drinks the day-moon
*

reeds, woodstuff, biter

Beach-glass

a redwing blackbird
down on the head
leaves his sand-prints
on top my cap
as waves pound trees

the spine seizes
and passerby laugh
beach-glass creeps up
the rolling of pebbles
along the wave-battered shore

it's raining in bay view
and the clouds are coming
over the waves
eating the shore

The Watermen:
Door County Scenes

limestone, basalt
wade under cypress
over feldspar to shale
we'll move earth
like others, to make
a space to walk
*
sheer, clear light
fossils roll
on the shore. curdles
of water massage
earth's edge
and we will live
'til the sun sets
we are trapped
but the words are free—
*
claws on dirt
children play
with dead fish
like pets and puppets.
*
a barest trace
of light splayed
'cross miles of water
jupiter delayed,
hanging in the eye
lightning bugs waft
thru aspen leaves,
birch logs burn
tongue of flame
asleep, slugs

coiling green
girth 'round toadstool
stalks in darkness,
mycelial volvae
bursting moss,
virginia waterleaf
explodes stamens
in the night, and still
jupiter floods
the sky slowly,
slowly delayed
*

day cardinal chortles
over emergent gemmed
amanitas. play whist
listen
       to waves
               in the dark—
*

fern-field branching
for sun unimpeded
sand-ringed swales
of light, dappled
caressing the base
one dead aspen
fern-flanked as i
make my ablution
squat on the wet
sand, water
gathered in hands
*

a glimpse of black
boggy bottoms
where trails don't go
and always the desire
to take—thicket
thrushes coupling,
berate as i move
by the bank, mosquitoes
elated for a mammal
stream rushes on
pulling and shifting
sand
     stone
              leaflitter—
moss-burrow, new
eyeline. we are off
the trail now
fern-bank underfoot
enter creek-current
cool water
over rough sand
*

the proud, lone
iris, standing
trunks for beetles—
must watch our step

To a Whale Bobbing Rhythmically in the Surf

fisc flodu ahof on fergenberig;
warþ gasric grorn, þær he on greut giswom.

the fish piled up waters on faces of rock;
the fearsome king grew sad, swam on the shingle.

—Franks Casket

Incessant marine furling and unfurling,
two otters glistening oiled barges,
spiked fields of clawberry succulents,
ocean breeze, ropey roots,
moor in miniature of yellow flowers.
And you're away down in the cove,
deep-cut wales furrowing your belly,
white spattered tail sways and the bloat
of your corpse says no life is left
in you. Vultures won't yet alight
on your hide, but they ride the cliff currents
in the midday sun above and around
your watery limbs. Waves rotate your body,
your massive head a cold pivot:
the purple blossoms trembling hundreds
of feet above your freakish and lovely bulk.

Jefferson County Highway Lunes

the dark sky holding
harvest moon—
i learned of your death

*

you are luminous
my darksome
friend. be radiant

For My Father

—Lake Michigan, 6-27-20

Here in my shelter from the sun,
tree limbs lichen-caked,
undulation of the clear mind's ocean—
he's there walking above me.
His quiet walk in the air's dew,
elms and ash looming green shadow life,
on our fresh way to Stop-N-Go
two blocks over before cars begin.
We walk in the neon lights
and he pours the coffee from the glass pitcher—
slightest scent of scorch on the recycled air.
From here in my perch on the sea I see
him in my mind's eye, shifting coolly
to the raised counter, his small printed
styrofoam cup filled with alkaloids and water
steaming under its lid. And maybe we walk
straight home, newspaper under arm.
And maybe we walk past the old water quarry,
thru scrubby maple wood. Seeing
the whole world as snapping turtles
laze and logs slant from the surface.
And it was quiet, the quiet dream broken—
                                        cold water.

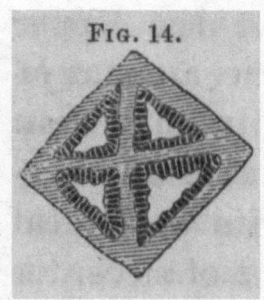
Fig. 14.

ii. Spring Ephemerals

For best work
you ought to put forth
    some effort
    to stand
in north woods
among birch

—Lorine Niedecker, "For best work"

Spring Ephemerals

Early Wisconsin conservationists Aldo Leopold, John Curtis, Norman Fassett, Cliff Germaine, and Albert Fuller saw the drastic altering and damage of land throughout Wisconsin and worked to preserve the remaining unaltered land they could find. Eventually their preservation of natural sites at the state level became Wisconsin's State Natural Area Program.

When COVID hit, I started a pandemic project travelling to State Natural Areas near my home. The plan was to visit a SNA, take a few pictures, and write a three-line "living found poem" about whatever we found there. It grew into an on-going, much larger affair than I suspected it would at first. This selection is the first slew of them, written from when the skunk cabbage was first coming up in March through when it had leafed out completely in June.

cudahy woods

shagbark hickory up the rise
skunk cabbage strains its spathe—
early risers awash in sun

warnimont bluff fens, a

your calcareous fens too rare
the dnr won't let us find you;
i respect the hell out of that

warnimont bluff fens, b

a hoary aspen clutches the gorge-side
as the lake's whisper breaks on the ear:
this sea will be here long after us

kurtz woods

hairy woodpeckers chasing thru beeches,
moss shrouds scarlet elf-cups—
a living world entire between

kewaskum maple-oak woods

in early spring sun
frogs croak in chorus
bloodroot stands in lobed splendor

milwaukee river floodplain and forest

a frog dives below the current
logcock sprints upstream
the river will not be stopped

jackson marsh, a

you point feverishly to warblers
as swifts swarm the marsh
trout lily is in bloom

jackson marsh, b

brilliant flash of orange
breaks over cedar creek:
your eyes against the sky

tichigan springs and fen, a

angled cluster of boughs
lain low among the pines—
red and mottled survivors

tichigan springs and fen, b

at the marsh edge
tussocks of moss watch,
rich with mucky life

tichigan springs and fen, c

the redwing blackbirds live
in a world all their own
cattails and fen-reek curve,
cradling the earth's bounds

bratt woods, a (supplementum series)

the trout lily's retired for the year
trillia haunt the ridges
heart speaks to heart

bratt woods, b (supplementum series)

lurking the mudstones
carp ride the tide
tanagers look on in silence

donges bay gorge, a (supplementum series)

wild turkey up the gorge
forget-me-nots support the sky
the mind saturated by oak

donges bay gorge, b
  (supplementum series)

springs seep from the bluff-face
over east-soil baking in sun
rivulets and restless children

man mound park (supplementum series)

man mound's horns
appropriately ferned
in spring rain

the lower narrows

the bluff scarred yet beautiful
bedraggled columbine hanging red
i must weep for very life

durward's glen (supplementum series)

we spook a blue heron
treading up prentice creek
stone streaming to pebble

riveredge creek and ephemeral pond, a

sedge sings out in tussocky throbs
to lonely kettle's close
skunk cabbage now green parasols

riveredge creek and ephemeral pond, b

riveredge creek slinks on
rivulets run like a web
while silent iris strains

A Cry of Lunes

moraine lune

below the cedars,
liverwort
in gravel and roots.

*

december lune

snowfall makes rivers
after dark
present to the eye

*

vigils word-lune

new life stirs the mind,
my early vigil:
reading proust 'til sleep comes.

*

i-94 east lune triptych

i.

ohio turkeys
glistening
in afternoon sun

ii.

white slashes scattered
on the page
of this stranded snag

iii.

purple loosestrife clings
to limestone
in frilled defiance

*

benedictine lune

i feel like st. ben
in deep need
of a thorn thicket

*

redwood lune

beneath the sorrel:
flapping moth
savaged by barred wren

*

big sur lune

silent ocean's self
down below
playing mockingbird

*

empire prairie lune

all the shrews and mice
just hoping
no kestrel unskies

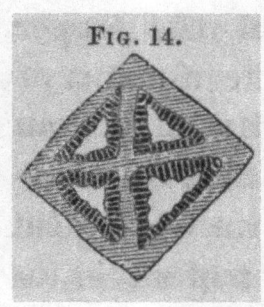

iii. Lows/*Hlæwas*

Nearly landless and on the way to water
I push thru marsh.
I lost a view . . . I saw

—Lorine Niedecker, "For Paul"

Deer Camp

For the Late Woodland cousins

New beech suckers lunging from old roots,
April sun growing stronger—
it's nursing bone and nets of clay
season after season in this clearing.
Lousewort sprouting, trees have no time,
only the *hrusan* they cling to, shout from.
Twilling of warblers thru the bare canopy
sonic waterfalls in limpid branches.

Playing hooky for kids' spring break,
skunk cabbage miracles abound
along the wetland lowland basin.
Water springs in dark channels
down to Hartman Creek, gray sand-banks
the Woodlanders used to found the effigies.

The heart-scent of dried leaves
among the moss-bound trunks in the lazing breeze
more evocative than any tea-dipped madeleine.
Kids scout ahead and tumble in the sticks,
always calling, already breathing earth.
Water spirits gather round our legs,
rogue daffodils nestled at the base
of the short ridge cleanse our minds
to see the ground, know the Deer—*heort*—
inhabiting this ground. The Treaty of the Cedars
let this land and severed ties,
a heron sprung from the shoreline with a blast
of feather and beak and leg.

The Ruin

*A translation of the Old English poem before
a Middle Woodland burial mound near Lake Michigan*

This soil-mound is wondrous, stranded by progress:
the city's encircled the survival of first peoples.
Tumuli erased, effigies plowed under,
soil has been scraped and frost fastly clings,
guards against chaos have been shorn, collapsed,
undercut by time. Earth-grasp clutches
the work's master—withered and rotted—
the ground's hard-grip, 'til a hundred generations
of that people have perished. For long this pile—
moss-hoary, weed-blotched—one town after another
endured under storms, steep and ample.
The low-place still wears away, hewn by weapons,
rests on the earth, its offing broken,
grimly ground down, the ground swallowed
it all . . . it shone . . .
. . . the skilled ancient shape . . .
. . . bowed in mudcrust . . .
. . . a mind dreamt up that thought-swift design,
strong-counsel of soil-rings, with spirit bound
the foundations together wondrously with dirt.
Bright were the villages, barrows surrounding,
tall with houses, great human sound,
many feasts held and filled with every joy,
until mighty fate made an end of that.
Slaughtered men fell, plague-days festered,
and death seized them, the bravest men.
Their defenses became desert places,
the village languished. Those sent to revive,
armies, died too. The dwellings fell,
their rectangular roofs rotted to nothing,
bark and stock. The mound stands above the plain,

its ruined peers broken like so many people,
once glad and splendid, adorned in splendor,
bold and haughty, who shone in their ornaments,
gazed on pottery, pipe bowls, treasures,
on bounty of copper and bone and slate,
on the bright barrows of this broad village.
The earth-mounds stood, the stream ran down
the bluff to the lake, embraced it all
in its bright bosom, where the houses stood
warm within. That was a delight.
Then they shed . . .
over hard stone, the holy streams . . .
. . . until the round pool. . . . Hot . . .
. . . where the water spirits lay.
Then . . . is . . .
. . . That is a powerful thing,
how the . . . mound . . .
   —Lake Park, Milwaukee, 2018

Intaglio

Fort Atkinson, WI

the rock river urges
grass-covered bank
water panther tracks

The Kviða of Helgi Hundingsbane (Final Scene)

From the Old Norse

At dusk, Sigrun's bondwoman went by Helgi's mound and saw Helgi riding into the mound with many men. The bondwoman said:

"Is this some deception it seems I see,
or the Ragnarok? Dead men riding,
where do you speed your horses with spurs,
or are you heroes given a longing for home?"

Helgi said:

"This is no deception you seem to see,
nor the opening of an age, though you perceive us.
Though we speed our horses with spurs,
now we heroes are given a longing for home."

The bondwoman went home and told Sigrun:

"Out you go, Sigrun of Sefafell,
if you'd try to find the lord of troops.
The mound is opened—Helgi is here!
Sword-tracks bleed, and Dag's own son
asks you to make well his bleeding wounds."

Sigrun went into the mound to Helgi and said:

"Now I'm as glad at the gift of our meeting
as the greedy hawks of grim Odin
when they smell slaughter, the warm corpses,
or, dew-glinting, they see daybreak.

"First, I would kiss the lifeless king
before you cast off that bloody byrnie.
Your hair, Helgi, is thick with rime,
the chief is all stricken with slaughter-dew.
Hogni's kinsman has cold, damp hands.
Speak to me, prince: how I can help you?"

Helgi said:

"You alone are the cause, Sigrun of Sefafell,
that Helgi the stern is stricken with grief-dew.
You cry, gold-adorned, with your grim tears,
sun-bright south-maid, before you go to sleep.
They fall bloody on the warrior's breast,
spray-cold, burning, filled with sorrow.

"Well, we should drink dear strong draughts,
though we've lost pleasures and lands.
No man alive should recite a sorrow-song,
though on my breast I bear these mortal wounds.
Now, this woman is immured in the mound,
a human woman with we who are passed."

Sigrun prepared a bed in the mound.

"Here I've made ready a bed for you, Helgi.
Much freed of angst, son of Ylfings,
I long, my lord, to sleep in your embrace,
as I would with the prince when he was awake."

Helgi said:

"Nothing at all could be less likely,
soon or late at Sefafell,
than you asleep in lifeless arms,
delicate in the mound, Hogni's daughter—
and you, breathing and royally born.

"It's time for me to ride the reddened paths,
to set the pale horse tredding the skyway.
I have to west over windhelm's bridge,
before Salgofnir wakes those who've won victory."

Helgi and his men rode off, and the women went back home. The next evening Sigrun had her bondwoman keep watch at the mound. And at dusk, when Sigrun came to the mound, she said:

"He'd have come by now, if he meant to come,
Sigmund's son from Odin's halls.
Any hope the lord will come hither wanes.
Now on the ash-limbs the eagles sit,
and all the folk flock to the dream-thing."

The bondwoman said:

"Don't be so bold as to go alone,
noble woman, into that ghost-house.
Stronger become all things at night,
dead enemies, by far, than by the light of day."

Sigrun did not live long after that, on account of her sorrow and grief. There was a belief in the old days that people could be born again, which is now considered an old wives' tale. Helgi and Sigrun were said to be born again. He was called Helgi Haddingjaskati, and she was Kara Halfdanardottir, as is told in the "Song of Kara," and she was a valkyrie.

Weland the Smith

From the Old English Meters of Boethius

Where now the bones of wise Weland,
the great goldsmith whose renown stretched wide?
I say "the bones of wise Weland"
for no earth-dweller can deny another
whatever skill Christ secured for him.
As difficult as it is to dislodge the sun
and the swift heavens from their proper circuit:
that's how hard it is for anyone to deny
another man his native skill.
Who can make out in what earth-mound
lay the bones of wise Weland,
strewn and stretched over the barrow's floor?
. . .

Though you ween and desire as well
that you'll press on living for a prolonged period,
why is that better—what makes "longer" best?
For death skips over not a single person
(though one's day-count seems to dally),
once it's been given the Lord's own leave.
What will anyone enjoy on that day,
a mortal from that fame, if immutable death
must seize his life after all his delights?

Leads and Diggings:
A Conglomerated Narrative

*"O! Lord! If you are the One who shows mercy on the poor,
then I am the poor one."*
—Tulsidas, trans. V.K. Subramanian

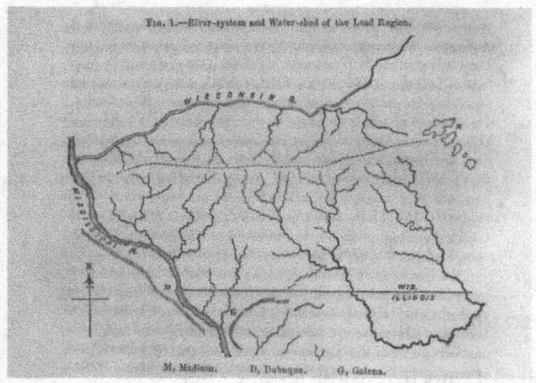

A note on sensitive material: Though poets' intentions may have little to do with how their work is read, I want to be as transparent as possible due to the sensitive nature of some of the material I work with here. In imagining (based in archival and oral history) my own family's coming to the Midwest from Europe, I do not mean to explain away or ignore the history of the forced removal and hostile treatment of Wisconsin's and Illinois's indigenous peoples. I plainly acknowledge their egregious mistreatment—in which my own ancestors were complicit—by the US government, state governments, and private citizens, without these realities being the specific aim of the poem's narrative.

A note on meter: All but the sections dealing with time periods before 1500 AD are in a syllabic meter found in Middle Cornish, an alternating count of seven- and four-syllable lines.

I. The Poetics of Extraction

> Physical and mental strength waste away together beneath accumulating years, and the memory of names, dates, and important events become buried in the confusion brought by time and its restless, unceasing changes. Circumstances that were fresh in memory ten or twenty years after their occurrence, are almost, if not entirely, forgotten when fifty years have gone, and if not entirely lost from the mind, they are so nearly so that, when recalled by one seeking to preserve them, their recollection comes slowly back, more like the memory of a midnight dream than of an actual occurrence in which they were partial, if not active, participants.
>   -H.F. Kett, 1878

Janesville, 2007

North Franklin Street comes alive
in powder blue,
a slow and humid morning.
As the same folks saunter in
the Sizzlin' Grill welcomes them
into its narrow doorway,
decades of cigarette smoke
defying the smoking ban
and eggs already frying.
Molly climbs the squat stairway,
grasping the wall for support,
her white curls rebounding from
the humid air.
She plops down at the table
north of the door.
Nancy pours her black coffee,
already placed the order
for her biscuits and gravy.
She looks down at the speckled

white china between fingers,
the rim circled,
and memory swims inside,
the outwash fan's outer edge
pragmatically paved behind
her rounded back—
the gravel and sandy till
that made up the glacier's gift
to the Rock's mouth:
ancient current preparing
home for burr oaks and prairie.
Coffee bitter on the tongue.

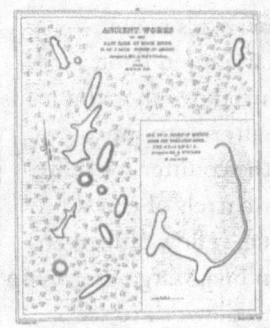

*

Vinegar Hill, 1933

Great Grandma Schaeber winces
at the bell's sound
as the door slams to behind.
Uncle Emerson leans down
slipping chocolate
down from the oakwood shelving
into Molly's girlish hands.
Great Grandpa James had passed on
ten years before
but Emerson kept it up.
All along the wood-plank walls
chest-height barrels
and her eyes running over
red and black beans
echoing the river's name,
potatoes darker and light,
dust floating above them light
in the late afternoon sun.
She scans the counter for more,
small stout barrels of candy,
red and blue, yellow and green.
Great Grandma Margaret gets up
from her needlework to see
Elizabeth,
to hear the news from Janesville.
And past the northern hollow
lays Hazel Green,
over Wisconsin's border.

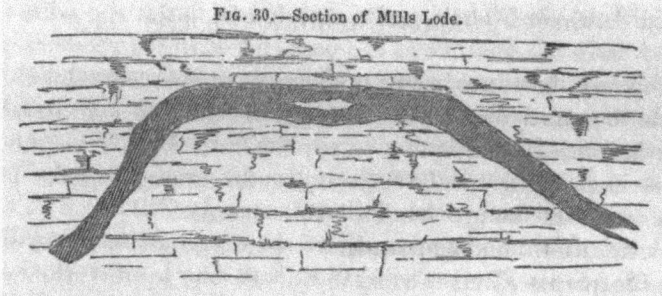

FIG. 30.—Section of Mills Lode.

Snakes sunbathe in the cornfields'
naked furrows,
the broken earth seeking rain.
Elizabeth's eyes look down
and her glance betrays concern
for her son the steeplejack
who walks on rooftops to feed
his small family,
looking over the tree-tops
thru the scent of tar paper.
Aunt Sara has brought in grapes
from her arbor
and she lays three bunches down
in Grandma's arms.
Elizabeth steps back out
and loads fat jars of honey
and honeycombs
into Emerson's wagon,
for she has brought him the fruits
of her orchard.
Each one chooses an apple
and all their teeth cut the skin.
Sunbeams thru the willow leaves,
and it's time to be on home.
*

Vinegar Hill, 1865—Ludwig Schaeber

"Oh, no, no, I come up here
years ago now.

"From Württemburg—
still a duchy when I's born.
Ah, me and Christiana
got here 1834,
two years after Blackhawk's War
it was now, yes.
Blackhawk stopped down the Fever
in September,
but they wouldn't come ashore.
Some of the Manns tried to see
him and couldn't.
But he was in Galena.
Frightful thing that war, all told—

"Oh, yes, that's the old mine shaft.
When we first got here you just
dug down into a hollow,
one man digging in the hole,
another hauling it up
with a windlass.

We were always looking for
the mineral,
but the limestone that whinnies
up out the ground along here,
it's fine for cellar walls, piers,
bridges and all,
though it must be dressed a bit.

"No, our diggings are all in
Vinegar Hill.
We've been down on Rocky Road,
mining crevices, not flats,
not like up at Hazel Green.
We've done all right by and bye,
though nothing like Owen's strike:
huge thing back in '28.

"We've about forty lodes here
in the township.

"Hmm? I's in Philadelphia
on my way here.
Curious thing for a kraut
like me, I'll say.
But once we got the diggings
we put ourselves on a whim
and have made a decent crack,
with farming year 'round as well.
Min'ral, blackjack, and chickens
we live on here.

Zinc	66.37
Iron	.79
Sulphur	33.41
Insoluble	trace.
	100.57

Ah, it's hard work sure enough,
the back and shoulders groan in't,
but this is what we have, now.
And can you imagine, now,
what it's like to walk along
the Fever River at dawn,
off for fishing,
seeing jack-in-the-pulpit
nestled there still in its leaves
below old oaks?
And to know that I'll die here?
To the ground with the min'ral
waiting long on the Final
Coming, I will.
And that's a fact."
*

Stratford, 1910

Three men there making music
tired on the porch
of dying beams.
A fiddle, flute, and guitar,
their caps slanted,
waistbands impossibly high,
anger and desperation
too hard to hide
in gaunt faces.
What song left their strings and lungs
under the sycamore trees,
shining in their Sunday best?
*

Vinegar Hill, 1851—
Alice Thomas Hocking

"No, we arrived recently,
we're miners and farmers all,
right down the line.

"Yes, this will be number six,
the first born here in the States.
My John's already fifteen,
almost out on his own now,
though we'll miss him when he's gone,
make no mistake—
thinking of Scales Mound, he is.

"Why, we left Gwillanwarthas—
that's near Camborne—
and sailed six weeks to Quebec.
Ah, the silence belowdecks
in the dead night on the seas,
leaving the old world behind!
And mid-passage I gave birth,
aye, but she didn't survive,
did all we could.
Poor girl is below the waves,
in the middle Atlantic,
God keep her soul.
A fine passage otherwise,
but the stench, well...
When once we were ashore there,
we crossed Lake Ontario
to Kingston, where we nearly
lost little Tom.
But we come to Buffalo,
and from there to Chicago.
Then it was on across land
to Galena.

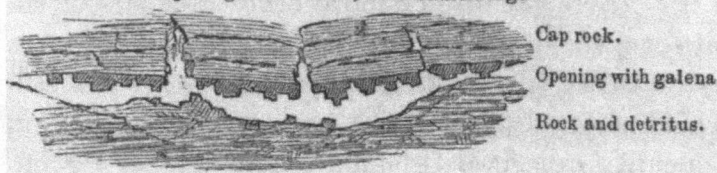

Fig. 24.—Flat Opening with Galena, near Shullsburg.

Cap rock.
Opening with galena.
Rock and detritus.

"Plenty of Cornishmen here
to help us in settling in.
And now a house,
the garden coming in well.
The diggings keep us afloat
here, every one.

"No, I don't suspect I will
see Britain or Kernow more.
The Northwest it is for us,
the Fever River and mounds,
nodding golden jewelweed blooms
in the evening's ragged sun."
*

Millbrig Hollow, 1885

Sitting on the riverbank
Louis fishes,
back against pine,
lure in the rippling water.
What does it matter if he
catches dinner?
This is time for rest from work
at the plough, winnowing fan,
winch and windlass,
whatever there is to do.
And the leaves are changing shade,
they fall on his short lapels.
And what's Katherina at?
Doesn't she know his hearing's
worse and worse now?
He served in the great war there
away into Tennessee.
Fighting didn't do him in,
but he drank the Tennessee
river's water in late March—
measles and diarrhea:
that rash drilled red all over,
nights in the heat with fever,
dehydration,
days not knowing if he'd live,
if he'd see his firstborn son
who'd been born in September,
if his eyes would ever look
on the Fever's softing banks
or sands again,
catching crayfish in the mud,
walking thru stands of yellow
trout lily blooms.

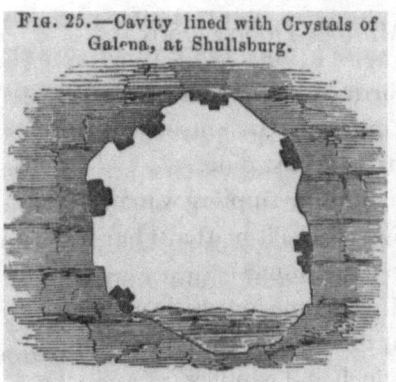

FIG. 25.—Cavity lined with Crystals of Galena, at Shullsburg.

But here he is,
years before the firing squad
let hammers bring his salute
graveside down in Galena.
Here he sits in the hollow,
bone and flesh against the dirt,
sunlight dappling the Fever
low and golden.
*

II. The Night Heron's Call

>   *Before the melt-waters*
> *had drumlin-dammed a high hill-water for the water-maid*
> *to lave her maiden hair....*
> *Long long ago they'd turned the flow about.*
> *But had they as yet morained*
>   *where holy Deva's entry is?*
> *Or pebbled his mere, where*
>   *still the Parthenos*
> *she makes her devious exit?*
>   —David Jones, *The Anathemata*

Between the Mississippi and Lake Michigan, anytime in the later Holocene

The black-crowned night herons hunt,
stalking the ripe water's edge.
Their feet women's elegant
skeleton hands
reaching for a fine dainty
deep in the muck.
*

Shallow Ocean,
 ca. 460-420 million years ago

liverworts luxuriate
with bryophyte kin,
enzymes shattering
rocky coastland
as millipedes
savage a newly
predatory
world. *cooksonia*
stretch their stalks
to open skies,
vascular tissues
transporting water
in the rivers' deltas.
but in the waters,
the waters shallow
and infused with light,
euroamerica
is coming together:
untold numbers
of bryozoans
and cephalopods
live and eat
and die in their millions,
leaving carbonate
deposits, and wind
and water and weight
do their work,
great gray clouds
move over the waters,
metallic salts
hang suspended

as sulpheretted
hydrogen
precipitates lead,
shapes sulpherrets
forming limestone:

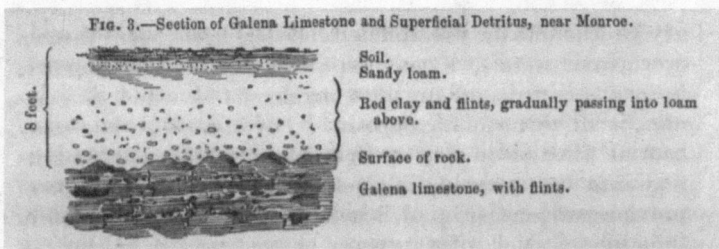

compacts, lithifies,
the sun across the sky,
earth orbiting
as joint crevices
fill, dolomite
drums clayey
deposits, yellow
and tough, immense
cogs crystalize
as limestone ions
dance with abandon,
dolomitization
drawing, lurching
forward so slowly,
like sugar and brown,
seawater bathing
marine sediments,
receptaculites
colonizing
the ocean benthos,

brachiopods
latched to seabed.
galena fills
crevices, lays out
in flats and pitches,

FIG. 22.—Flat sheet with Galena, at Bracken & Allen's Mine, Mineral Point.

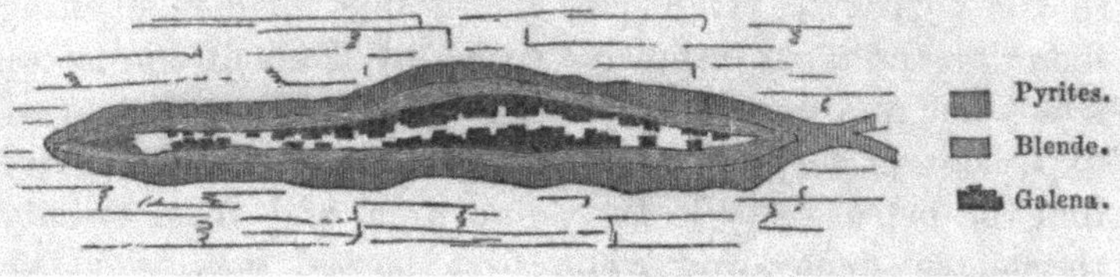

ordovician
mineral rest
on beds of passage
into the drab
and buff as zinc
oxidizes
to sphalerite.
mud piles
and piles to shale,
a strangulation.
for now, the waves
play on, crashing
into the growing shore,
a millennial tick:
the waters subside.
*

*The Confluence of the Yellow and Mississippi Rivers,
 ca. 1,000 years ago*

They're carrying clay and ochre up the sandstone,
buckets and buckets of soil under the hardwoods,
over the dolomite's curves and bluff slopes.
Fingers of prairie grass meet the woods
away below, and muscles heave their loads.
The Great Bear is taking splendid shape.
Soon it will grow with woodland grasses, under stars.
It will gaze across the Great River
long after these artists have gone beyond the waters.
*

Man Mound Park, 2018 and ca. 1,000 years ago

gray autumn skies spread memory round about,
heavy stands of barberry on raised tussocks
under oaks. a sleeping sentinel ringed round
by drumlins, moraine, blanketed by this small field
of blossoming clover slumbering and soft to the touch,
the rounding folds of his body breaking angular at the joints.
lostness clings like lichen, the pearled clouds pass by.
a maimed, wandering spirit on the move and planted
here for a thousand seasons between Bede and Ælfric
plying their monkish trade in scriptoria a world away.
great horned form straitened by the sepulcher white
of asphalt at the knees. his bed the rhyolite earth,
its clothes detritus of hazelnuts and double-serrate
leaves in fivefold clusters, horns wreathed in fern
and goldenrod, creeping jenny trailing and sneaking
through grassy allies spurting from fragrant soil.
a sole vulture glides overhead marking out his length,
and shocks of cool purple michaelmas daisy lay
on fernish ground while bovine sentries toss their heads
in the mud rollicking and mounting. his city mosquito-speckled

maples, cottonwoods dropping new decay to the earth
and the ribald smell of good dark humus.

o horned spirit, what words did they say to you?
what were their supplications?
whose vision did they follow to sculpt your
protean, graceful form, walking westward,
head to the halfway line of the world, feet
to its top? what lies within and beneath you,
manmund, werhlæw?

iube Domine silentium fieri in aures audientium,
ut possint intelligere et Deo benedicere

iube, Domine, benedicere
   * * *

they will build you, bucketful after bucketful
of soil lain over ash and cist gathered
at your heart in the midmorning gold—
not too much from one place, lest a canker
be left open, a breach in the topsoil.
the Lower Narrows visible in the gaps between maples
the cornfields emerging, fires have been burning,
charcoal left to marble atop multi-colored soils.
they lay you straight and solitary
to hold this place,
clusters of rock beneath your cranium,
the upper world made in earth relief,
and so we are, and so you stand until the earth
is no more.

iube, Domine, benedicere
*

Carwynnen, ca. 3,900 BC

The granite is up, Cambrian intrusion's darling
localized here as the Carnmenellis pluton.
The batholith rolls and spoils in Neolithic
rainfall. Megacrystic capstone shelters
the workers as they lay granite and quartz
for circling and leading pavements, looking north.
One looks skyward and eyes the killas, marks
of heat and touch. They've not come far, but heavy
work hoisting the *cromlech* fine. Soon
acids will do their eating act, this dolmen
will fall one day. But now the props are up,
soon they'll loom over smoldering bones like a spider,
when they start the oak-logs burning, and gather
the ashes and char, tender, in gabbroic pots.

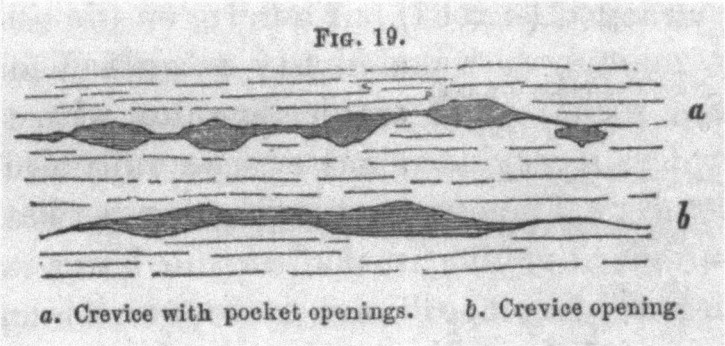

a. Crevice with pocket openings.   *b.* Crevice opening.

When camp is broke they'll march back to the Crooked Hill
across the streams that become Dowr Koner.
But first, they must heap earth, thick earth
over the leavings of those gone before,
around the sockets, over the dolmen's reach:
a bare mound to say that they were here.
*

*Rock River Valley below Lake Koshkonong,
ca. 16,000-13,000 years ago*

freezing and thawing
freezing and thawing
freezing, thawing—
ice thick
and dense, receding
slowly from this place.
hundreds and hundreds
of miles the ice
has lumbered granite,
copper, clays,
sand and gravel,
the water pours
and gushes and wells,
floods and flows
off the icesheet,
thru tunnel channels
and boring eskers
cutting clean
caves of mass.

here one channel
and another over
the already ancient
riverbed.

every day
the streams sluice
more sand and gravel
out in pristine
unconsolidated fans.
grains of silica
torrents of silt
tumble cobbles
and erratic boulders
into deep deposits,
orderly, stratified,
homely but powerful.
the plains will grow
with grass and flowers,
blue stem
and blazing star.
bees will come
and frogs to the kettles.
bison will range
and herons will fish
on the heated back
of the glacier's remains.
humans will come.
skunk cabbage
will lay claim
to spring soil,
and bloodroot too.
oak and hickory
tamarack and pine.
bogs will glory
and fens be born
from springs in what
ice left behind.
muskrats will make

their pushups and swim
in the free marshes.
flat expanses
will shelter corn
and tobacco. ridges
rising up to the north
and the east, ground
moraine cushioning
the frozen corridor
to the final fall,

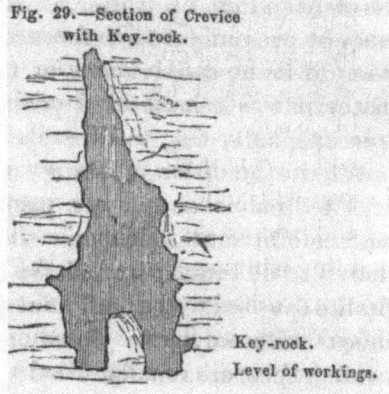

a gentle descent
to river's course,
overlapping
sandstone and limestone
from earlier sea
bottoms and all
moving, every
last piece.
and Love will look down and smile.
*

Marquette County, 2020

First you're skirting the tree-line,
you the graceful silhouette
in the gloaming
above the still lake's water.

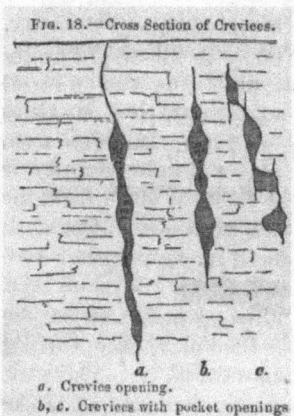

You are the dark bird, green bird
with red eyes, the lake itself
and the lilies, the birch stand
and the drowned marsh.
*

III. The Lions of Time

He talked about persistence,
a congruence of lives…
    —Seamus Heaney, "Belderg"

Milwaukee, 2020

Looking stops the shaft of mind,
photons and inks
at work on eyes, softeners
riding the lions of time.
There is something I've not known.

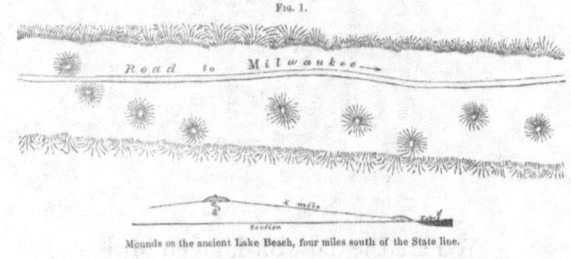

Go down, but wait
for lower angled sunlight.
We know the water, we know
the river's edge.
Spanned and splayed across state-line,
haunting the Fever River,
kissing the Rock
with bared hands and corduroy.
Molly will tell us it all—
The name was and is *Schaeber*.
We dream our night
and I will deny myself
all legitimate pleasure
to look squarely in your eyes,
to look and dream.
*

Gwillanwarthas, 1841—Thomas Hockin

"Alice—what's to be done, love?
This lean-to can't stay our home.

"Chipped china here, strewn on cloth,
we see tea leaves make their way
into veins of blood of tin
and the Merrygeeks will leave:
cowed shanty town ringed 'round rock
straddling great dragons of ore.

"Gwillanwarthas is no place
for us no longer, my dear.
Away: to where I know not.

"Margaret not yet a twinkle
in an eye, sun going down.
Who will linger in Camborne,
now that its mines find no tin?
Away, away 'cross ocean,
grandfathers' watches, hair pins,
scattered lithographs and night
falls, industry sick at heart."
*

Philadelphia, Oct. 7, 1828—
Ludwig Schaeber

"There's a good vegetable soup
with a hambone
we had earlier today,
away up Sassafras Street.
Have you seen Washington Square
before today?

"It's my first time.
I heard it was terrible,
a potter's field before this,
yellow fever.
But my, the sky is blue here!
Some of the leaves fallen now—
who'd have thought it?

"Yes, we made our way thru the
Lazaretto yesterday.

"Oh, no, I was a tailor,
specialized in corduroy.
I suppose there's call for clothes
in this place too:
jackets and slacks and waistcoats.
I'll ply my trade by and bye,
and teach my young Karl here too.
I figure we'll stay on here,
tho' there was mining back home,
and I hear tell of diggings
in the Northwest.

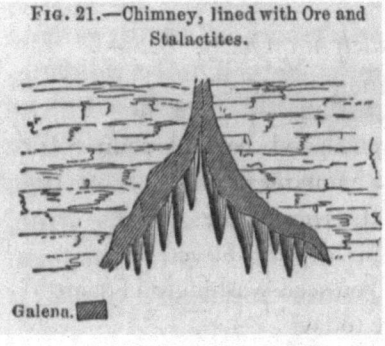

Fig. 21.—Chimney, lined with Ore and Stalactites.

Galena.

"The Black Forest, if you'll know,
the Black Forest was our home.
The Schaebers have always lived
in the Schwarzwald.
We've been heaving up the lodes
of lead and zinc
along the Enz for years on.
You've never seen a forest
like the Schwarzwald, I'll tell you.
When you see the early sun
thru the boughs in Waldrennach
where Christiana grew up,
or my village Conweiler,
those rolling hills
plotted thick with conifers—
or the fine meadow grasses
of small Dennach
from where all my grandsires hail—
there you touch the face of God:
Abnoba, naked water,
Diana's bathing altar.
But the Manchester brought us
all the way from Le Havre—
Normandy was grand to see—
and we'll have to get along.
At least there's land to be had.
I've a meeting with some folk
tonight to see where we'll go.

Pardon, could I trouble you
for a matchstick?"
*

Durward's Glen, 1866

Back from conglomerate cliffs,
layers of pressured quartzite,
beneath the pines,
men are building a chapel.
Free-stone succumbs to hammers,
dragged by oxen
and piled, masoned, lifted high:
four rubble walls to contain
the altar of Sacrifice,
Melchizedek's
bread and wine will be raised up,
the high places
provide fitting enclosure.
Margaret looks on,
rigid like a post beneath
a tall white pine,
as David and Gordon climb
the rubble walls
to complete the Gothic roof.

The steeple and shingles and
white cross will burn.
But today there is sunshine,
there is laughter and thrush-song.
Prentice Creek runs in the glen,
and Bernard can't stop writing
and looking forward fondly
to the day the Eucharist
graces this hill,
hillside calling to hillside,
in this tabernacle made
of living stone.
Hammer on nail echoes out
in all directions at once.

*

Janesville, 2020

She's there still pacing the lawn—
a hundred and fifty years
in her pocket:
a leaden ball,
mined ore of generations.
This folk, this place,
this awesome river valley,
all great aunts and abusings,
crumbling streets and commercial
developments.
Geese feeding beneath dead trees
in empty fields.
Mom and Dad off and away
months at a time—
to Newville and Edgerton,
further up the watershed
up to refuge.
Family terrible branches
spreading thru taverns and sun.
But this city on the Rock
alone is home.

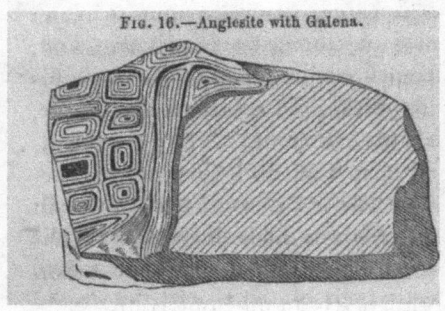

FIG. 16.—Anglesite with Galena.

Sandhills stand tall in marshes,
the homing counties today
their call to generations.
O, look to the clouds above
the Rock River,
and know. And know.
O, look to the clouds above
the Rock River,
and know. And know.

They said to one another,
we'll pave the trails,
the Sauk and Winnebago—
a great network
spanning marsh and field and glen!
The deer will keep themselves clear
of these highways.
And now the beaver are gone,
and the elk and buffalo.
And from this very valley,
and others too,
they pushed them out—
the Ho-Chunk, the Sauk and Fox—
to Nebraska, Iowa,
and to Kansas.
Some travelled back
again and again. Some stayed;
many did not.
Latter-day apologies
cannot change what happened then.
Violence is a long, long train
of many cars.

Great God! Who could have dreamt up
this slow horror?

And this little plot above
the gravel pit
will have to do.
The rattle-call of sandhills
is heard away by Spring Brook,
water and sediment all
off to the Rock.
*

IV. Till and Beds

> Del ony onen ha try
> Tas ha map yn tynyte
> Ny a'd wra ty then a bry
> Haval d'agan face whare
> Ny a whythin thy vody
> Sperys may hylly beuse
> Ha'n bewnans pan y'nkylly
> The'n dor ty a dreyl arte.[1]
> ~Anonymous, *Ordinale de Origine Mundi*

December 2020, along Highway 51

Their pale shades haunt the cornfields.
We ride the plain with outwash,
fan ridges east,
on our way to Kidder Road,
jog to the left
in the lightly blowing snow.
Up Manogue to Bill Fiedler's,
Clara's brother,
Sandy Sink Cemetery
on the small knoll
where she spent her open time.
The blades are off the windmill
in the cold air—
a tripod of weathered wood
high above Thresherman's Park.
    * * *

---

[1] From the Middle Cornish mystery play, when God makes and Adam and says: "As we are one and three, / Father and Son in Trinity, / We make thee, man, of clay, / Like to our face, presently. / We breathe into thy body / A spirit that thou mayest live, / And the life when thou losest it, / To the earth thou shalt turn again" (57-64; trans. Edwin Norris).

Here in the sleet-strewn ruins
of an old watering hole
on the highway,
shadows of women and men
assault the mind—
brick chimney sixteen feet high,
box of St. Peter's sandstone
quarried eagerly down road,
a fine pitched roof,
wooden shingles splintering
curved in sunken collapse of
a century,
the plain tile floor turned to scrub,
weed, and gravel.
Bill sat just here.
And so did Hum.
And maybe they didn't know
what else to do,
grown 'round now by thorn and grass.
Just 'round the bend on Hurd Road
Lou farmed long across the street
where Bill laid logs on the tracks
one sad, gray night,
geese crossing the moon-fed sky.
    * * *
Tobacco grows broad and green
on ground moraine
back to 1854,
small acres about the plots
where Fiedlers were laid to rest—
here's Samuel and Augusta,
and William and Augusta—
and sandhills call overhead,
on the watch for grain to glean.

The Ruosches asleep southward—
John and Bertha, and Gertrude,
George. And Louise
on Rollin Street,
the regal line of birches.
Around the curve on Broadway
my aunt had her heart broken
by her father
who came in quiet one night,
said he was leaving her mom,
and left his ring.
She and her little brother.
The memory still made her cry
in the year before her death
at ninety-four.
Grandpa John across the street
hewed and polished, bent the wood
to form a wraparound porch—
the first there in Edgerton—
above the moving water,
always the moving water,
brown and liquid and alive:
Saunders Creek a force marching
down into the Rock below
Indianford.
She is a part of this earth.
Albert oversaw all this
as park superintendent,
toiling in the embrace of
Cream City brick.
* * *

A lone grave but new headstone—
Otter Creek Cemetery,
where Willie's bones are sinking
into dark earth,
hummocky moraine edging
a farmer's field.
His wife and lover and child
became earth in other homes.
And the windmill's blades are gone.
*

Below Fulton, early 1800s

Here is our Ur-Surveyor,
bending geometry to
empire's purpose:
lines and boundaries.

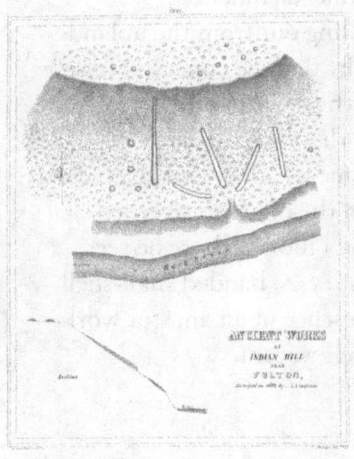

His hat lies in the grasses,
a welter of intentions
and assumptions play inside
the gray matter
of the Land Ordinance's
greatest high priest
(in the old Northwest at least).
Theodolite poised keenly,
he triangulates the ground,
the Yahara flowing by
and into the confluence
with the Sinnissippi flood
tumbling down from Horicon,
the Bark and Crawfish mixed in
this deep valley.
Lapham spies these tumuli
at the head of a glacial
tunnel channel
rolling out from the uplands.
Why does he concern himself
with present antiquities?
With mounded earth,
home to bones and layered clay?
On the blackish riverbed
not a foot offshore he sees,
surveys, a banded snail-shell—
presence of an ancient work
itself, vacant.

Fig. 10.

Row of Mounds near Fulton.

*

Milwaukee, 2020

When I was a child, my friend
lived on Blackhawk.
I never thought much of it.
It T'd on Clark Street, my street,
and when it rained
a glorious flood would form
at the pavement's confluence—
and we would splash and exalt
in the downpour
while downhill in the valley
the Rock River
sang, O, the glory of God
and he used to plant his corn.
*

Johnson Hill Kame,
   Sheboygan County, 2021

When we read nature's book, we
do well to recall we read
the reader too.
*

December 4, 1962, Edgerton

The warped porch boards are painted
a chalky blue,
the paint is thick.
Cinderblocks support her chair
and a small table laid out
with almond sugar cookies
and black coffee
in neat mugs of porcelain.

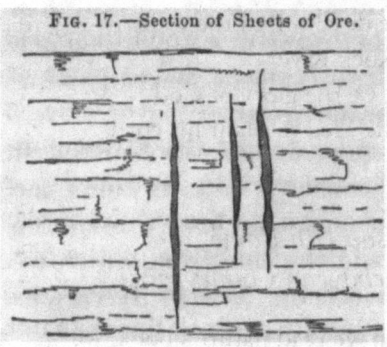

The screen door shuts with a bang
long and lovingly practiced.
Louise steps out on the lawn,
hangs black stockings on the line
on Rollin Street.
Later she'll walk down Chaucer
to Saunders Creek
to listen to the water
bounce gently along the shore
and watch the ducks.
Back past Clara's house, Clara
who will hold a baby just
before she dies—
Louise will not get the chance.

On this day she remembers
the horror that came for her
older sister and her child
down highway across the Rock,
and she hopes for Clara's kids,
standing beneath the elm trees:
that they will smile
and watch the waters run by
as herons call from the banks,
that these people will find joy
and not more pain.
But pain will come,
as will the night heron's call.
*

Maple Creek, 1881

Here in the winding bottoms
the trout lilies are in bloom.
And Gaudenz loves to come here,
to this swamp oak
to look at the Embarrass,
just to watch water slip by
on its way down to the Wolf.
The riverway overlaps
in mind with the Rabiusa
raging on below Malix
northeast of the Bärenhorn.
These flat floodplains
and ground moraine,
silver maples and green ash,
the ericaceous bogland
across Highway 54,
have made a new home for him,
fringed with oxbows.
A waterthrush's flight song
saturates the evening air
as Gaudenz Ruosch looks downstream.
Soon his bones will rest westward
in a small plot
north of County W.

His bent frame leans on the oak
for its support,
the bank pitted, with some give
against his linen shirtsleeve.
And who can explain this dream
of total movement onward?
His gray eyes angle up from
under his hat
to view purple ribs of sky.
*

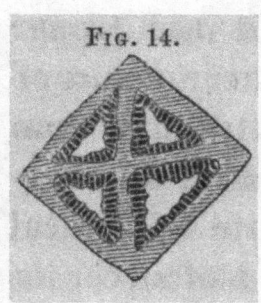
Fig. 14.

iv. The Monadnock Apostrophes: Baraboo Hills, Wisconsin

We are what the seas
have made us

longingly immense

—Lorine Niedecker, "We are what the seas"

i. The Rock Hermitage, Durward's Glen

> *"No one can be so imprisoned or so tightly guarded*
> *that he cannot find a way out from time to time."*
> —Marie de France, "Milun" (trans. Burgess)

This day surely will fly by—
a heron on the wing down Baraboo's river.
O Hermitage! Your small, white-washed innards
wrap us up. Who could live
here all Wisconsin-winter long
not going mad for the sight of them?
And Boo down the hill keeps the grounds
as we listen to birdsong thick
and undulating like the striped wings
of a pileated woodpecker, bluffs
to the left, bluffs to the right, and holy—
lovely rhyolite and quartzite striations
filling and framing and holding the brain.
Fan blades cut the air over Precambrian
pink Baraboo quartzite rock-ribs,
and we make coffee where Father John
used to celebrate Mass in your defunct oratory.
And we hermits pray and gaze and read,
we make love in the star-filled night.
You watch over us all as the glen
falls into deep. Calming of frog-croaks
and a clear sky to the Milky Way
as we escape the tyranny of billboards.

ii. Baxter's Hollow

Down your asphalt gullet we go.
Miles of one-and-a-half lane road,
no shoulder, few turnoffs. Into Baxter's Hollow,
birds luxuriating in your unbroken tree-blanket
remnant of le Grand Bois, the Big Woods
of hickory and oaks red and white,
basswood. White pines crouch
on the stream banks, waiting. We march single file
where a path used to lie, tussocky and tick-lined,
savage anthills a horror to look upon!
Your outwash, your pressed grasses and brush
under canopy a bear to walk thru, lighting out
down nontrail after nontrail and this Wisconsin wilderness
halts us reluctant after ten yards—
the most pathetic naturalists to visit
in years. Jack-in-the-pulpit, bear corn,
large-leaved aster, witch hazel
shape your understory with leather-tough wood fern,
partridgeberry. We happen on an old
foundation with its steps—what did they say
to each other closed in by all this
vegetation? We dream deciduous
dreams, Otter Creek—you benevolent overlord,
seeing all, watching over this
from your boulders as we turn our steps from sprawling
lily-of-the-valley on the loose for a century.
And you keep us out of your hollow, you resist us
in our lack of necessity. And you chuckle good-naturedly,
for your flowers and glories, your spring-beauty trillium,
your marsh marigold and shooting-star are safe.

iii. Alpine Diner

Here's the square up from St. Joseph's
with its oddly effeminate paramour in stained glass
I used to watch with wary eyes all Mass.
And we're looking for you, Alpine, standing there
on Fourth Street in your vernacular brick for decades
in rain and snow and sun. We met when
my grandfather was still here, but he's gone
for years now; you endure. Mammal
heat and '30s wooden molding
frame each booth's recessed cavern
and then your victuals pour out the kitchen,
numb anxiety with starch, caffeine,
and six-egg omelets to turn the earth
on its axis. An infinity of mirrors recurring
our relief on and on below farm-themed
knick-knacks. You've done it again, Alpine:
readied us for daylong hikes and mound-hunting,
for quartzite-climbing and setting by lakeshores.
And here we sit, eternal diner
of the mind, awaiting our flight
thru plate-glass and brass from your dreaming warmth.

iv. Pewit's Nest

How many times have I passed by
your humble turnoff? Past your
vulnerable flanks? Your beauty?
To see your recesses, I must lean out
over mud-brown water—strain to get
the eye-line matched to your crevice-curves,
the torrent of form, ripple of wave
in Skillet Creek under your low-slung passes,
precarious on your stepping stones.
The gorge quietly thunders
as the Northern Cardinal sings
up in the hemlock, red cedar—
the elm knows what it wants.
And they're climbing your sandstone,
the boot-press displacing soil
clung to your Cambrian side
for millennia. Trampled fences,
blight of humans, a network
of premeditated garbage
coming to rest in your potholes,
circling your yellow birch fingers.
I hope they rip out your road,
gravel your asphalt parking lot,
plant over your paths, make
them lost to time forever
like the mill that once sat on your banks.
Let them hide you from us—we don't
know how to love you as we ought.

v. The Lower Narrows

the Baraboo with its steep banks
lumbers thru your inviting limbs
and she is born as we are born
a passage of life and death, terrible
and bountiful at once. i passed the Fox,
the Rock and Crawfish, the broad Meskonsing
to be here with you, here at the bottom
of an ancient sea, dried up and haunting
gate to a mountain range worn
and worn by the years, by sand, by water
worn. my grandparents lived here in your ring,
one of them died here too, in earshot
of your river. but the rain drives the fog
over your bluffs and i place my hands
on wet rhyolite's ridges, hear
the hillsides singing, raindrops falling
into the swollen streams with their mournful
music. and in this gorge you place
my heart on your rocky altar, an offering
burnt of childhood and dream, clear-eyed
mortality and joy here in the narrows.
here in your shadow where the dark gray
of your sky teaches life itself,
filling the hollows, the glens. i've driven
down these roads glowing rose
and you speak to me, my kids, just as
you spoke to those before, vaunting
stone and whelming water in your wisdom.

+PAX-INTER-SPINAS+

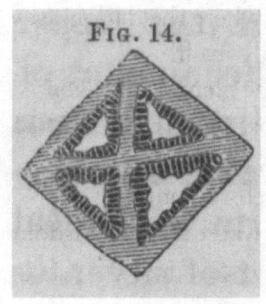

Fig. 14.

Acknowledgments and Thanks

Poems presented here have appeared in the following generous journals and magazines: *Presence, Hummingbird Magazine, Spirit & Life, Amethyst Review, The Cabinet of Heed, Exchanges, Saint Katherine Review, Macrina Magazine, Bez & Co., The Marquette Literary Review, Green Ink Poetry, Dappled Things, The Solitary Plover, The Tide Rises, the Tide Falls, boats against the current, Solum Journal, Riverbed Review, Better Than Starbucks, Wild Roof Journal, Paddler Press, Magpie Lit, Grand Little Things, Adversus Press, Wild Roof Journal, The Brazen Head*, the chapbook *The Covid Verses, Ballast Journal, The Crank, The North American Anglican, The Broken Spine*, and *Foxglove Journal*.

Printed images are culled from J. D. Whitney's *Report of a Geological Survey of the Upper Mississippi Lead Region* (Albany, 1862) and I. A. Lapham's *Antiquities of Wisconsin* (Washington, D.C., 1855). Thanks to Marquette's digital librarian Max Gray and digital programs technicians Leslie Quade and Ian Ruedinger at Raynor Library for help transferring images.

Original prints by the author in imitation of various early medieval English artefacts, an event in the life of St. Benedict, and contemporary plants found in southeastern Wisconsin.

Special thanks to everyone who has visited Wisconsin's State Natural Areas with me since the pandemic began—Mamie, Clara, Selevan, and Abram (who were there at the start); Paul, Kim, and Dave (who pressed on); Jerusha, Mike, Jennifer, David, and more. We walk the earth together.

TITLE INDEX

A

A Cry of Lunes 56
Alpine Diner 116
A Pentecost Sonnet 37

B

Baxter's Hollow 115
Beach-glass 42
Below Fulton, early 1800s 105
benedictine lune 57
Between the Mississippi and Lake Michigan,
    anytime in the later Holocene 83
Big Sur 28
big sur lune 58
Bogquilt 30
bratt woods, a (supplementum series) 54
bratt woods, b (supplementum series) 54

C

Carwynnen, ca. 3,900 BC 89
cudahy woods 52

D

December 4, 1962, Edgerton 108
December 2020, along Highway 51 102
december lune 56
Deer Camp 62
De nominibus 15
donges bay gorge, a (supplementum series) 54
donges bay gorge, b (supplementum series) 55
Durward's Glen, 1866 98
durward's glen (supplementum series) 55

E

empire prairie lune 58

F

Fen and Fastness: Images 41
For My Father 48
Freude: On Hearing Beethoven's 9th Symphony
    after a Two-Year Pandemic Delay 36

G

Gwillanwarthas, 1841—Thomas Hockin 95

H

Haight Pome 29
Holy Resurrection Monastery 40

I

i-94 east lune triptych 57
Intaglio 65

J

jackson marsh, a 53
jackson marsh, b 53
Janesville, 2007 72

Janesville, 2020 99
Jefferson County Highway Lunes 47
Johnson Hill Kame, Sheboygan County, 2021 107
June Sketch 38

K

kewaskum maple-oak woods 53
kurtz woods 53

L

Lake Michigan Gied 21
Leads and Diggings: A Conglomerated Narrative 71

M

Man Mound Park, 2018 and ca. 1,000 years ago 87
man mound park (supplementum series) 55
Maple Creek, 1881 110
Marin 27
Marquette County, 2020 93
Martin's Woods 33
Millbrig Hollow, 1885 81
Milwaukee, 2020 .... 94, 107
Milwaukee Protests June, 2020 24
milwaukee river floodplain and forest 53
moraine lune 56
Morning Snow 18

O

Old Growth 14
On Being the Tooth Fairy 39
On First Concert at the
    Bradley Symphony Center, Milwaukee 25
On Free Organ Concerts in
    Milwaukee's East Village 32
On Having a Daughter 23
On Knowledge and Love 19

On Picking a Spotted Touch-Me-Not 34
On Reading the Biography of Henry I: A Triolet 35
On the Year's First Compost 17

P

Pewit's Nest 118
Philadelphia, Oct. 7, 1828—Ludwig Schaeber 95

R

redwood lune 58
riveredge creek and ephemeral pond, a 55
riveredge creek and ephemeral pond, b 55
Rock River Valley below Lake Koshkonong,
    ca. 16,000-13,000 years ago 90

S

Shallow Ocean,
    ca. 460-420 million years ago 84
Sketch for Desert Fathers 26
Spring Ephemerals 52
Stratford, 1910 78
Submission 22

T

The Confluence of the Yellow and
    Mississippi Rivers, ca. 1,000 years ago 87
The Kviða of Helgi Hundingsbane (Final Scene) 66
The Lions of Time 94
the lower narrows 55
The Lower Narrows 119
The Night 31
The Night Heron's Call 83
The Poetics of Extraction 72
The Rock Hermitage, Durward's Glen 114
The Ruin 63
The Watermen: Door County Scenes 43

tichigan springs and fen, a 54
tichigan springs and fen, b 54
tichigan springs and fen, c 54
Till and Beds 102
To a Whale Bobbing Rhythmically in the Surf 46
To the Milwaukee, Downtown 16

V

vigils word-lune 56
Vinegar Hill, 1851—Alice Thomas Hocking 79
Vinegar Hill, 1865—Ludwig Schaeber 76
Vinegar Hill, 1933 74

W

warnimont bluff fens, a 52
warnimont bluff fens, b 53
Weland the Smith 69

First Line Index

A

a frog dives below the current 53
a hoary aspen clutches the gorge-side 53
Alice—what's to be done, love? 95
all the shrews and mice 58
angled cluster of boughs 54
a redwing blackbird 42
A solitary tom strolls 19
At dusk, Sigrun's bondwoman went by Helgi's mound .. 66
at the marsh edge 54

B

Back from conglomerate cliffs 98
below the cedars 56
Beneath an afternoon sun 23
beneath the sorrel 58
blue goose road at night 30
brilliant flash of orange 53
broadsides stapled to telephone poles 31

C

chaotic flurry 18

D

dark canyon walls shining moonglow 22
Down your asphalt gullet we go 115

F

first cool breeze of summer 38
First you're skirting the tree-line 93
Free organ music here 32
freezing and thawing 90

G

gray autumn skies spread memory round about 87
Great Grandma Schaeber winces 74

H

hairy woodpeckers chasing thru beeches 53
Here in my shelter from the sun 48
Here in the winding bottoms 110
Here is our Ur-Surveyor 105
Here's the square up from St. Joseph's 116
How many times have I passed by 118

I

i feel like st. ben 57
Incessant marine furling and unfurling 46
in early spring sun 53
In the failing evening's light I read 35

L

limestone, basalt 43
liverworts luxuriate 84
logs drowning 33

Looking stops the shaft of mind 94
lurking the mudstones 54

M

man mound's horns 55
milwaukee's smell 24

N

New beech suckers lunging from old roots 62
new life stirs the mind 56
North Franklin Street comes alive 72
No, we arrived recently 79

O

O Edward Elgar, did you see our faces 25
ohio turkeys 57
Oh, no, no, I come up here 76
once you had banks 16

P

Paul the hermit in his desert 26
purple loosestrife clings 57

R

riveredge creek slinks on 55

S

sedge sings out in tussocky throbs 55
shagbark hickory up the rise 52
She's there still pacing the lawn 99
silent ocean's self 58
Sitting on the riverbank 81
Sleet and stiff breeze cold about the ears 14
snowfall makes rivers 56
South of Port des Morts we find ourselves 37
springs seep from the bluff-face 55

T

talking virgins over crepes 29
the Baraboo with its steep banks 119
The black-crowned night herons hunt 83
the bluff scarred yet beautiful 55
the children open eyes wide 17
the dark sky holding 47
the dollar bill refuses to yield 39
The granite is up, Cambrian intrusion's darling 89
the hall lined with cyrillic inscriptions 40
Their pale shades haunt the cornfields 102
The man swiveling disembarks 28
The master couldn't hear his work 36
the redwing blackbirds live 54
There's a good vegetable soup 95
the rock river urges 65
The towhees are singing their whirring song 27
the trout lily's retired for the year 54
The warped porch boards are painted 108
They're carrying clay and ochre up the sandstone 87
This day surely will fly by 114
This orange-speckled cup 34
This soil-mound is wondrous, stranded by progress 63

U

up from the fen sedge 41

W

We argue about bellwort in this late-night 15
we're digging sand and stone at the shore 21
we spook a blue heron 55
When I was a child, my friend 107
When we read nature's book, we 107
Where now the bones of wise Weland 69
white slashes scattered 57
wild turkey up the gorge 54

Y

you point feverishly to warblers 53
your calcareous fens too rare 52

www.ingramcontent.com/pod-product-compliance
Lightning Source LLC
Chambersburg PA
CBHW011328190426
43193CB00047B/2925